# STUDY PLANNER

D -

| MOOD ☺☺☺☹☹ | DATE. | | MON | TUE | WED | THU | FRI | SAT | SUN |
|---|---|---|---|---|---|---|---|---|---|

**TODAY'S PRIORITY**

○

○

○

| PLAN | | | TOTAL TIME | H | M |
|---|---|---|---|---|---|
| | | ○ | | | |
| | | ○ | 6 | | |
| | | ○ | 7 | | |
| | | ○ | 8 | | |
| | | ○ | 9 | | |
| | | ○ | 10 | | |
| | | ○ | 11 | | |
| | | ○ | 12 | | |
| | | ○ | 1 | | |
| | | ○ | 2 | | |
| | | ○ | 3 | | |
| | | ○ | 4 | | |
| | | ○ | 5 | | |
| | | ○ | 6 | | |
| | | ○ | 7 | | |
| | | ○ | 8 | | |
| | | ○ | 9 | | |
| | | ○ | 10 | | |
| | | ○ | 11 | | |
| | | | 12 | | |
| COMMENT | | | 1 | | |
| | | | 2 | | |
| | | | 3 | | |
| | | | 4 | | |
| | | | 5 | | |

# STUDY PLANNER

D -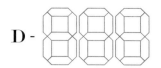

| MOOD ☺☺☺☹☹ | DATE. | | MON | TUE | WED | THU | FRI | SAT | SUN |
|---|---|---|---|---|---|---|---|---|---|

**TODAY'S PRIORITY**

- ○
- ○
- ○

| PLAN | | TOTAL TIME | H | M |
|---|---|---|---|---|
| | ○ | 6 | | |
| | ○ | 7 | | |
| | ○ | 8 | | |
| | ○ | 9 | | |
| | ○ | 10 | | |
| | ○ | 11 | | |
| | ○ | 12 | | |
| | ○ | 1 | | |
| | ○ | 2 | | |
| | ○ | 3 | | |
| | ○ | 4 | | |
| | ○ | 5 | | |
| | ○ | 6 | | |
| | ○ | 7 | | |
| | ○ | 8 | | |
| | ○ | 9 | | |
| | ○ | 10 | | |
| | ○ | 11 | | |
| | | 12 | | |
| | | 1 | | |
| | | 2 | | |
| | | 3 | | |
| | | 4 | | |
| | | 5 | | |

COMMENT

# STUDY PLANNER

| MOOD ☺☻☺☹☹ | DATE. | MON | TUE | WED | THU | FRI | SAT | SUN |
|---|---|---|---|---|---|---|---|---|

**TODAY'S PRIORITY**

- ○
- ○
- ○

| PLAN | | |
|---|---|---|
| | | ○ |
| | | ○ |
| | | ○ |
| | | ○ |
| | | ○ |
| | | ○ |
| | | ○ |
| | | ○ |
| | | ○ |
| | | ○ |
| | | ○ |
| | | ○ |
| | | ○ |
| | | ○ |
| | | ○ |
| | | ○ |
| | | ○ |
| | | ○ |
| | | ○ |
| | | ○ |

| TOTAL TIME | H | M |
|---|---|---|
| 6 | | |
| 7 | | |
| 8 | | |
| 9 | | |
| 10 | | |
| 11 | | |
| 12 | | |
| 1 | | |
| 2 | | |
| 3 | | |
| 4 | | |
| 5 | | |
| 6 | | |
| 7 | | |
| 8 | | |
| 9 | | |
| 10 | | |
| 11 | | |
| 12 | | |
| 1 | | |
| 2 | | |
| 3 | | |
| 4 | | |
| 5 | | |

**COMMENT**

# STUDY PLANNER

D -

| MOOD ☺☺☺☹☹ | DATE. | | MON | TUE | WED | THU | FRI | SAT | SUN |
|---|---|---|---|---|---|---|---|---|---|

**TODAY'S PRIORITY**

○

○

○

| PLAN | | | TOTAL TIME | H | | M | |
|---|---|---|---|---|---|---|---|
| | | ○ | | | | | |
| | | ○ | 6 | | | | |
| | | ○ | 7 | | | | |
| | | ○ | 8 | | | | |
| | | ○ | 9 | | | | |
| | | ○ | 10 | | | | |
| | | ○ | 11 | | | | |
| | | ○ | 12 | | | | |
| | | ○ | 1 | | | | |
| | | ○ | 2 | | | | |
| | | ○ | 3 | | | | |
| | | ○ | 4 | | | | |
| | | ○ | 5 | | | | |
| | | ○ | 6 | | | | |
| | | ○ | 7 | | | | |
| | | ○ | 8 | | | | |
| | | ○ | 9 | | | | |
| | | ○ | 10 | | | | |
| | | ○ | 11 | | | | |
| | | | 12 | | | | |

**COMMENT**

| | 1 |
|---|---|
| | 2 |
| | 3 |
| | 4 |
| | 5 |

# STUDY PLANNER

D -

| MOOD ☺☺☺☹☹ | DATE. | MON | TUE | WED | THU | FRI | SAT | SUN |
|---|---|---|---|---|---|---|---|---|

**TODAY'S PRIORITY**

- ○
- ○
- ○

| PLAN | | | TOTAL TIME | H | | M | |
|---|---|---|---|---|---|---|---|
| | | ○ | | | | | |
| | | ○ | 6 | | | | |
| | | ○ | 7 | | | | |
| | | ○ | 8 | | | | |
| | | ○ | 9 | | | | |
| | | ○ | 10 | | | | |
| | | ○ | 11 | | | | |
| | | ○ | 12 | | | | |
| | | ○ | 1 | | | | |
| | | ○ | 2 | | | | |
| | | ○ | 3 | | | | |
| | | ○ | 4 | | | | |
| | | ○ | 5 | | | | |
| | | ○ | 6 | | | | |
| | | ○ | 7 | | | | |
| | | ○ | 8 | | | | |
| | | ○ | 9 | | | | |
| | | ○ | 10 | | | | |
| | | ○ | 11 | | | | |
| | | | 12 | | | | |
| COMMENT | | | 1 | | | | |
| | | | 2 | | | | |
| | | | 3 | | | | |
| | | | 4 | | | | |
| | | | 5 | | | | |

# STUDY PLANNER

| MOOD ☺☺☺☹☹ | DATE. | MON | TUE | WED | THU | FRI | SAT | SUN |
|---|---|---|---|---|---|---|---|---|

**TODAY'S PRIORITY**

- ○
- ○
- ○

| PLAN | | | TOTAL TIME | H | M |
|---|---|---|---|---|---|
| | | ○ | 6 | | |
| | | ○ | 7 | | |
| | | ○ | 8 | | |
| | | ○ | 9 | | |
| | | ○ | 10 | | |
| | | ○ | 11 | | |
| | | ○ | 12 | | |
| | | ○ | 1 | | |
| | | ○ | 2 | | |
| | | ○ | 3 | | |
| | | ○ | 4 | | |
| | | ○ | 5 | | |
| | | ○ | 6 | | |
| | | ○ | 7 | | |
| | | ○ | 8 | | |
| | | ○ | 9 | | |
| | | ○ | 10 | | |
| | | ○ | 11 | | |
| | | | 12 | | |
| | | | 1 | | |
| | | | 2 | | |
| | | | 3 | | |
| | | | 4 | | |
| | | | 5 | | |

**COMMENT**

# STUDY PLANNER

D -

| MOOD ☺☺☺☹☹ | DATE. | | MON | TUE | WED | THU | FRI | SAT | SUN |
|---|---|---|---|---|---|---|---|---|---|

**TODAY'S PRIORITY**

○

○

○

| PLAN | | | TOTAL TIME | H | | M | |
|---|---|---|---|---|---|---|---|
| | | ○ | | | | | |
| | | ○ | 6 | | | | |
| | | ○ | 7 | | | | |
| | | ○ | 8 | | | | |
| | | ○ | 9 | | | | |
| | | ○ | 10 | | | | |
| | | ○ | 11 | | | | |
| | | ○ | 12 | | | | |
| | | ○ | 1 | | | | |
| | | ○ | 2 | | | | |
| | | ○ | 3 | | | | |
| | | ○ | 4 | | | | |
| | | ○ | 5 | | | | |
| | | ○ | 6 | | | | |
| | | ○ | 7 | | | | |
| | | ○ | 8 | | | | |
| | | ○ | 9 | | | | |
| | | ○ | 10 | | | | |
| | | ○ | 11 | | | | |
| | | | 12 | | | | |
| **COMMENT** | | | 1 | | | | |
| | | | 2 | | | | |
| | | | 3 | | | | |
| | | | 4 | | | | |
| | | | 5 | | | | |

# STUDY PLANNER

| MOOD ☺☺☺☹☹ | DATE. | MON | TUE | WED | THU | FRI | SAT | SUN |
|---|---|---|---|---|---|---|---|---|

**TODAY'S PRIORITY**

- ○
- ○
- ○

| PLAN | | | TOTAL TIME | H | M |
|---|---|---|---|---|---|
| | | ○ | | | |
| | | ○ | 6 | | |
| | | ○ | 7 | | |
| | | ○ | 8 | | |
| | | ○ | 9 | | |
| | | ○ | 10 | | |
| | | ○ | 11 | | |
| | | ○ | 12 | | |
| | | ○ | 1 | | |
| | | ○ | 2 | | |
| | | ○ | 3 | | |
| | | ○ | 4 | | |
| | | ○ | 5 | | |
| | | ○ | 6 | | |
| | | ○ | 7 | | |
| | | ○ | 8 | | |
| | | ○ | 9 | | |
| | | ○ | 10 | | |
| | | ○ | 11 | | |
| | | | 12 | | |
| | | | 1 | | |
| | | | 2 | | |
| | | | 3 | | |
| | | | 4 | | |
| | | | 5 | | |

**COMMENT**

# STUDY PLANNER

D -

| MOOD ☺☺☺☹☹ | DATE. | MON | TUE | WED | THU | FRI | SAT | SUN |
|---|---|---|---|---|---|---|---|---|

**TODAY'S PRIORITY**

- ○
- ○
- ○

| PLAN | | |
|---|---|---|
| | | ○ |
| | | ○ |
| | | ○ |
| | | ○ |
| | | ○ |
| | | ○ |
| | | ○ |
| | | ○ |
| | | ○ |
| | | ○ |
| | | ○ |
| | | ○ |
| | | ○ |
| | | ○ |
| | | ○ |
| | | ○ |
| | | ○ |
| | | ○ |
| | | ○ |
| | | ○ |
| | | ○ |

| TOTAL TIME | H | M |
|---|---|---|
| 6 | | |
| 7 | | |
| 8 | | |
| 9 | | |
| 10 | | |
| 11 | | |
| 12 | | |
| 1 | | |
| 2 | | |
| 3 | | |
| 4 | | |
| 5 | | |
| 6 | | |
| 7 | | |
| 8 | | |
| 9 | | |
| 10 | | |
| 11 | | |
| 12 | | |
| 1 | | |
| 2 | | |
| 3 | | |
| 4 | | |
| 5 | | |

**COMMENT**

# STUDY PLANNER

D -

| MOOD ☺☻☺☹☺ | DATE. | MON | TUE | WED | THU | FRI | SAT | SUN |
|---|---|---|---|---|---|---|---|---|

TODAY'S PRIORITY

○

○

○

| PLAN | | | TOTAL TIME | H | M |
|---|---|---|---|---|---|
| | | ○ | | | |
| | | ○ | 6 | | |
| | | ○ | 7 | | |
| | | ○ | 8 | | |
| | | ○ | 9 | | |
| | | ○ | 10 | | |
| | | ○ | 11 | | |
| | | ○ | 12 | | |
| | | ○ | 1 | | |
| | | ○ | 2 | | |
| | | ○ | 3 | | |
| | | ○ | 4 | | |
| | | ○ | 5 | | |
| | | ○ | 6 | | |
| | | ○ | 7 | | |
| | | ○ | 8 | | |
| | | ○ | 9 | | |
| | | ○ | 10 | | |
| | | ○ | 11 | | |
| | | | 12 | | |

COMMENT

| | | |
|---|---|---|
| 1 | | |
| 2 | | |
| 3 | | |
| 4 | | |
| 5 | | |

# STUDY PLANNER

D -

| MOOD ☺☺☺☹☹ | DATE. | MON | TUE | WED | THU | FRI | SAT | SUN |
|---|---|---|---|---|---|---|---|---|

**TODAY'S PRIORITY**

○

○

○

| PLAN | |
|---|---|
| | ○ |
| | ○ |
| | ○ |
| | ○ |
| | ○ |
| | ○ |
| | ○ |
| | ○ |
| | ○ |
| | ○ |
| | ○ |
| | ○ |
| | ○ |
| | ○ |
| | ○ |
| | ○ |
| | ○ |
| | ○ |
| | ○ |

| TOTAL TIME | H | | M | |
|---|---|---|---|---|
| 6 | | | | |
| 7 | | | | |
| 8 | | | | |
| 9 | | | | |
| 10 | | | | |
| 11 | | | | |
| 12 | | | | |
| 1 | | | | |
| 2 | | | | |
| 3 | | | | |
| 4 | | | | |
| 5 | | | | |
| 6 | | | | |
| 7 | | | | |
| 8 | | | | |
| 9 | | | | |
| 10 | | | | |
| 11 | | | | |
| 12 | | | | |
| 1 | | | | |
| 2 | | | | |
| 3 | | | | |
| 4 | | | | |
| 5 | | | | |

**COMMENT**

# STUDY PLANNER

D -

| MOOD ☺☺☺☹☹ | DATE. | MON | TUE | WED | THU | FRI | SAT | SUN |
|---|---|---|---|---|---|---|---|---|

**TODAY'S PRIORITY**

- ○
- ○
- ○

| PLAN | | ○ |
|---|---|---|
| | | ○ |
| | | ○ |
| | | ○ |
| | | ○ |
| | | ○ |
| | | ○ |
| | | ○ |
| | | ○ |
| | | ○ |
| | | ○ |
| | | ○ |
| | | ○ |
| | | ○ |
| | | ○ |
| | | ○ |
| | | ○ |
| | | ○ |
| | | ○ |

| TOTAL TIME | H | M |
|---|---|---|
| 6 | | |
| 7 | | |
| 8 | | |
| 9 | | |
| 10 | | |
| 11 | | |
| 12 | | |
| 1 | | |
| 2 | | |
| 3 | | |
| 4 | | |
| 5 | | |
| 6 | | |
| 7 | | |
| 8 | | |
| 9 | | |
| 10 | | |
| 11 | | |
| 12 | | |
| 1 | | |
| 2 | | |
| 3 | | |
| 4 | | |
| 5 | | |

**COMMENT**

# STUDY PLANNER

D -

| MOOD ☺☺☺☹☹ | DATE. | MON | TUE | WED | THU | FRI | SAT | SUN |
|---|---|---|---|---|---|---|---|---|

**TODAY'S PRIORITY**

○

○

○

| PLAN | | ○ |
|---|---|---|
| | | ○ |
| | | ○ |
| | | ○ |
| | | ○ |
| | | ○ |
| | | ○ |
| | | ○ |
| | | ○ |
| | | ○ |
| | | ○ |
| | | ○ |
| | | ○ |
| | | ○ |
| | | ○ |
| | | ○ |
| | | ○ |
| | | ○ |
| | | ○ |
| | | ○ |
| | | ○ |

| TOTAL TIME | H | M |
|---|---|---|
| 6 | | |
| 7 | | |
| 8 | | |
| 9 | | |
| 10 | | |
| 11 | | |
| 12 | | |
| 1 | | |
| 2 | | |
| 3 | | |
| 4 | | |
| 5 | | |
| 6 | | |
| 7 | | |
| 8 | | |
| 9 | | |
| 10 | | |
| 11 | | |
| 12 | | |
| 1 | | |
| 2 | | |
| 3 | | |
| 4 | | |
| 5 | | |

**COMMENT**

# STUDY PLANNER

| MOOD ☺ ☺ ☺ ☹ ☹ | DATE. | MON | TUE | WED | THU | FRI | SAT | SUN |
|---|---|---|---|---|---|---|---|---|

**TODAY'S PRIORITY**

- ○
- ○
- ○

| PLAN | |
|---|---|
| | ○ |
| | ○ |
| | ○ |
| | ○ |
| | ○ |
| | ○ |
| | ○ |
| | ○ |
| | ○ |
| | ○ |
| | ○ |
| | ○ |
| | ○ |
| | ○ |
| | ○ |
| | ○ |
| | ○ |
| | ○ |
| | ○ |
| | ○ |
| | ○ |

**COMMENT**

| TOTAL TIME | H | | M | |
|---|---|---|---|---|
| 6 | | | | |
| 7 | | | | |
| 8 | | | | |
| 9 | | | | |
| 10 | | | | |
| 11 | | | | |
| 12 | | | | |
| 1 | | | | |
| 2 | | | | |
| 3 | | | | |
| 4 | | | | |
| 5 | | | | |
| 6 | | | | |
| 7 | | | | |
| 8 | | | | |
| 9 | | | | |
| 10 | | | | |
| 11 | | | | |
| 12 | | | | |
| 1 | | | | |
| 2 | | | | |
| 3 | | | | |
| 4 | | | | |
| 5 | | | | |

homepage      goseowon.com
blog      blog.naver.com/goseowongak
insta      @swk_book

인생에 뜻을 세우는데 있어
늦은 때라곤 없다.

볼드윈

**(주)서원각**

**대표번호** │ 02-324-2051
**교재주문** │ 031-923-2051
**홈페이지** │ www.goseowon.com
**주　　소** │ 경기도 고양시 일산서구 덕산로 88-45(가좌동)
**문　　의** │ 카카오톡 플러스 친구 [서원각]